SCORPIO HOROSCOPE
2015

Lisa Lazuli

Lisa Lazuli is the author of the amazon bestseller

HOROSCOPE 2014: ASTROLOGY and NUMEROLOGY HOROSCOPES

ABOUT THE AUTHOR

Lisa Lazuli studied astrology with the Faculty of Astrological Studies in London.

She has practiced since 1999.

Lisa has been a regular guest on BBWM and BBC Shropshire talking about astrology and doing both horoscopes and live readings. She has also made guest appearances on Fox FM, BBC Cambridgeshire, BBC Northamptonshire, BBC Coventry and Warwickshire and US Internet Radio Shows including the Debra Clement Show.

Lisa wrote horoscopes for Asian Woman Magazine.

Now available in eBook and paperback:

TAURUS: Your Day, Your Decan, Your Sign *The most REVEALING book on The Bull yet.* Includes 2015 Predictions.

ARIES HOROSCOPE 2015

TAURUS HOROSCOPE 2015

GEMINI HOROSCOPE 2015

CANCER HOROSCOPE 2015

LEO HOROSCOPE 2015

VIRGO HOROSCOPE 2015

LIBRA HOROSCOPE 2015

Lisa Lazuli is also the author of

The mystery/thrillers:

A Sealed Fate

Holly Leaves

Next of Sin

<u>As well as:</u>

Delicious, Nutritious Recipes for the Time and Cash Strapped

Paleo Diet: Get Started, Get Motivated, Feel Great.

99 ACE Places to Promote Your Book

Pressure Cooking Reinvented.

FOREWARD

Dear Reader,

I hope my yearly horoscopes will provide you with some insightful guidance during what is a very tricky time astrologically speaking with the heavy planets i.e. Pluto and Uranus at loggerheads in cardinal signs and Neptune in Pisces calling us all to get in touch with our spiritual side.

I have a conversational style of writing, please excuse any grammatical errors, I write much as I would speak.

As the song goes, "Nobody said it was easy." I know the mass media pump-out shows us plenty about quick fix love, money, fame and success; however, life is a journey filled with challenges and obstacles designed to encourage us to find out what we are made of and who we really are.

Embrace the good and bad and enjoy what is your unique experience.

Be the hero in your own personal life movie and never hide your spotlight.

I must add that the best astrology insights are gained from a unique chart based on your time, date, year and place of birth.

If you would like your natal chart calculated for FREE, click here:

http://lisalazuli.com/2014/06/30/would-you-like-to-know-where-all-your-planets-are-free-natal-chart/

Please join me on Facebook:

https://www.facebook.com/pages/Lisa-Lazuli-Astrologer/192000594298158?ref=hl

Contents

We hear so much talk of hard work, achievement, striving and struggling, and it is true that adult life is not for the faint-hearted, but 2015 is a year when Scorpio will wake up and smell the roses: it is a time of looking to enhance pleasure, beauty and comfort in your life and to appreciate relationships and friendships. It is a year of enriching experiences for you personally and enjoyable moments when you will feel warm inside as you relish the beauty all about you. 2015 presents an excellent opportunity for new love to blossom. No matter what you are going through right now, there is for sure a lighter side to 2015 and opportunities to enjoy life and feel good about yourself and your world.

You will think a lot about what you truly value in life and in people, and you will want to steer yourself towards life situations where you experience less stress and more pleasure – it's a year of asking, "What's it all about?" You will reassess your priorities and look to strengthen bonds with those that really matter and to make new friendships with people who can bring warmth and laughter into your life. Scorpios are known to be loners and when they choose friends they are discerning and prefer a small circle of really close friends rather than a large circle of social butterflies. However, this is a great year to make new friends, who will also be friends that last and friends who possibly better reflect where and who you are now than your current friends do. This is not a year to go it alone, team up with others and do not shy away from communal ventures to which you can contribute enormously.

You will certainly plan your year to include trips, excursions, days out, holidays and make more time for the hobbies and pastimes you enjoy most. If you once enjoyed sailing or sewing or delving into mysteries, you need to get back to that – this year make time for those activities that you thoroughly enjoy.

Scorpios are highly creative and in touch with their artistic side this year. You may well decide that you will throw yourself into redecorating your home, which will satisfy your need for beauty and comfort as well as exercising that arty gene you have. You want your life to be more organized and more convenient – you will de-clutter your home and workspace and cut out activities that hassle you and waste time. In Feng Sui, clutter in the home equates to clutter and confusion in the head – this year Scorpios are getting into a better head space by making their lives neat and streamline. This need for harmony extends to relationships with colleagues and neighbours, which you will seek to smooth over, getting rid of complications and needless antagonism.

You may feel inspired to take on a whole new look – getting rid of your old wardrobe and embracing a new, more vibrant way of dressing. You will look to dress and portray yourself in a way more reflective of who you are, and it will feel good – liberating. Looks matter to Scorpios, who are very good at staying young. Dr Chris Barnard (who did the first heart transplant in Cape Town) a Scorpio, said that aging was a disease. Gary Player and Tova Borgnine also Scorpios have been obsessive about fitness, looks and staying young. This year Scorpios will look towards diet, exercise and beauty products to enhance and extend their youthfulness. But feeling young is not always about face packs, diets and botox – it's about being happy and stress free. Negative emotions play out on the facial features; they drain us mentally and physically – this year the positive and loving vibes of Scorpio are radiating out and aiding the youthful appearance. On the theme of self-improvement, Scorpio may switch to organic food, take more supplements, avoid the sun, get more fit and in general think more about how you treat your body. It is not just a sudden interest in health; you want to look good and feel good about yourself and eating better, thinking positively and avoiding stress are all part of that.

2015 is a time when you can appreciate things and see the beauty in simple everyday moments – your ability to see past problems and assess the purpose and meaning in everything is enhanced. Your ability to give out love and warmth will ensure that family relationships are better than ever. Somehow because you are more comfortable within yourself it is easier for you to express emotion and love.

In business, this is a wonderful year for Scorpios involved in the fashion, beauty, hospitality, entertainment or the retail industries. However, in any line of business, there is money to be made, and this is a very financially rewarding year. Scorpios, who work in negotiating, politics, promotions, marketing and teaching will also be very successful. In all walks of life, you will seek to iron out discord and bring people together for pleasure and business. A very good year for mixing business with pleasure and hosting client events, launches, marketing drives and staff bonding weekends away.

When we are feeling good, we tend to do something … yes … spend! It is a side effect of feeling positive. Scorpios can earn well this year, but it may be going out as quickly as it is coming in. Do keep an eye on your finances this year and ask yourself, "Do I really need this?" Socially, you are far more active this year, which can be too much alcohol and party food – now while in general you are health conscious this year, your social calendar can make sticking to the health goals you have set yourself harder, so make time to detox in-between.

You are highly magnetic and attractive as well as generous emotionally, and this will make meeting new partners easy. Initially, it may be your suitor who is more infatuated with you than you with him/her. Sometimes, finding a line between friendship and love can be hard: you may feel it's friendship while the other person wants it to be love. Time will tell, as for you, you will have to wait and see if that friendship grows into love. There is no doubt that this year is one when cupid can strike, but you know what cupid is like; he's very muddled and love is often confusing in the first stages, especially when there is more than one potential mate vying for your attention. 2015 is a wonderful year to marry if you are already involved with someone.

Your emotions and passions are intense this year, if you do decided you like someone, you will be very amorous and can commit quite quickly, you will be eager for the relationship to devour you both and you can become quite possessive. You must try harder to be more objective in new love relationships.

In marriages and committed relationships, things should run smoothly, and you will have a good time together. Your faithfulness and loyalty will be as unquestionable as ever, even if you are a tad too intense at times. Scorpios do not hold back when their passions are aroused: those who hurt the ones you love will feel your sting big time. If you have been struggling lately, this is an ideal year to make a new start or to get some counselling, you are able to tackle the taboo subjects in your relationships now, and that aids truth seeking and healing. You can get things back on track if you are truly in love. However, since Scorpio are being very honest with themselves this year about what really matters and what really makes them happy, they cannot glue a bad relationship together for the sake of it – make a decision about what makes you happy, and go for it. If you can be happier and less stressed away from the relationship, have a break from each other or a trial separation – I don't think this is a year for radical decisions, a break apart may do the trick.

Sometimes Scorpios can be overwhelmed by the complex and powerful emotions which can engulf them, but this year, you will not be ignoring those emotions, but embracing and confronting them in a way that can take you forward in all your relationships. Scorpios need to look for the answers to why they react so explosively to certain things. What are your triggers? Why do you need to control certain things or situations? Scorpio tend to feel first, react and never ask, why? This year ask, why? Find out where your red lines are, and why you react as you do. Seek to understand yourself, and from there you can address issues or talk to your confidantes about how to deal with these emotions you have – in this way you can be less stressed and more comfortable with yourself.

This is a year of chapters firmly shut in terms of people you do not like: I once heard that Scorpio love 5% of people, hate 5% with a passion and couldn't give a damn about the rest. Well, this year the 5% you hate will feel the Siberian wind chill factor, and you are going to give the middle 90% a chance and surprise yourself.

This is a very good year for making decisions as you have the ability to be detached and impartial – often Scorpio go with gut feel, but 2015 is a very good year for lists, pro and con weighing and looking at things objectively. This objectivity is also wonderful for getting in touch with your own deeper needs and values and how to satisfy them.

You have a keen eye for beauty this year, and if you ever have wanted to know more about the arts, this is the time to pursue that as you are very aesthetically aware and able to appreciate the finer points of art and music, etc. An interest in culture and architecture may inspire many visits to galleries, museums or landmarks, or perhaps it will be the fabric markets of Mumbai or food markets of Bangkok which draw you – whichever way Scorpio are looking to indulge the senses and immerse themselves in sound, flavor, color and culture.

You are very practically minded this year, and for Scorpios who work (or partake in pastimes) in fields where art and method/maths/skill combine it can be very productive, i.e. architecture, landscaping, sculpture, haute couture, town planning, woodwork, pottery, jewelry making, etc. Scorpios are great with their hands, patient and determined, which means that they can excel in any form of craftwork. The more you enjoy what you do, the harder you will work, and you will see results. Scorpios are competitive this year and have a strong need to excel – you will work tirelessly to attain perfection in what you do and to create what you are proud of. A Scorpio's productivity and creativity are in direct proportion to the level of enjoyment and satisfaction you gain from what you do. Put your energy into what you do best and what you enjoy most, and the results will be stunning.

A positive energy imbues you with confidence this year and the ability to bounce back from and not dwell on hiccoughs. You can deal with setbacks and problems well, and they will not drain you nor inhibit your progress and feeling of personal power. Your sunny outlook will bring luck your way and problems should be resolved with little difficulty. With moderation and consistent effort, your achievements will really surprise you, and you can count on support and help from those around you when you need it. There is a sense of justice prevailing and good winning over bad in your life, and along with that you are inspired to be fairer and just in all your decisions and thoughts. This is not a year of vindictive or spiteful actions by you or towards you – it is a year to smooth over ill-feeling and to have a forgiving, forward-looking attitude.

2015 is a year of turnabouts – you can take a failing business, love life, career, health and turn that all about 180 degrees.

Sexually you are passionate and energetic, and your sex life will be more exciting and enjoyable than ever.

One warning this year is greed – you may be driven to do anything for money or prestige, and you could perhaps become an unashamed social climber and snob. I don't think I need to give you any more warning about this – the pitfalls are obvious. You will only fall into this one if your self-image is inextricably linked to wealth and material items due to a low self-esteem. It is, in this case, the low self-esteem which must be addressed. All that glitters is not gold, and greed often leads one to fall foul of the unscrupulous.

A year to stay away from crime hot spots and dodgy parts of town. Do not be tempted to deal in anything that is not 100% 'kosher'. Play it by the book.

2015 is a year of sheer determination, where you can get or achieve anything you want. Since you are more in touch with your inner needs and values, this should result in you achieving something of worth and lasting value. You have the willpower to break through barriers and the mental ingenuity to circumvent all obstacles in your way. You make an implacable opponent, and the best ally anyone could have in true Scorpio tradition this year. No one should underestimate Scorpio in 2015 as the power is with you, and the wind is in your sails.

It is not only holding your tongue but learning when to stay quiet – jumping in and saying something that either reveals too much or allowing something to slip out can lead to some embarrassment. Think before you speak, and remember that the less said about some things, the better.

It is a very busy month, but your memory is excellent and so your ability to observe and retain relevant fact and figures is enhanced. You can get more done this month if you work in solitude. Things are likely to be very hectic at home with relatives popping in or staying, and so if you do work from home you may want to head to a library or a friend's house for some peace and quiet so that you can get some quality work done and can concentrate properly. If you go out to work, you may decide to stay longer at work to avoid the hubbub at home. With Mercury going retrograde on the 22nd, you may experience issues to do with your home broadband or transport issues in your daily commute, so leave extra time and do not leave too many errands and business travel until the end of the month.

This is a pleasantly nostalgic month when you may reminisce with family about the old days – you may haul out the photo albums and trawl through them, telling your children more about your childhood.

You may decide to tidy out your basement or loft in order to create more space and to get organized – it may be a leak or water damage which precipitates this need to have a clear-out, but it can be a very good thing, and you will be amazed at what you rediscover as well as how much more space you free up.

This is also a month when you can improve your life by rediscovering a friend from the past or by talking or writing about your past – i.e. a blog about your town in your era.

Make sure this month you tie up loose ends – if there is something you have left undone, and that has nagged away in the back of your mind – use this opportunity to complete it and tick it off the list.

LOVE

A very good time to talk about issues of the heart as long as you do that before Jan 22 when Mercury turns retrograde. You should find it easy to express your emotions and needs within your love life. Single Scorpios will find it very easy to speak with their new lovers on an intimate level and as far as general banter goes.

After Jan 22, it may be harder to communicate effectively as you will tend to make too much of things and could end up in a drama about nothing. Your perspective is somewhat distorted, and you may focus on something unimportant, missing the essential issue.

Scorpios in new love relationships may find the romance very distracting and all-consuming, and you may struggle to think of anything else – in this way, matters of the heart may interrupt work and study. But often this kind of romantic distraction is just what we all need from time to time and it can be a great deal of fun.

Sex and love life is favoured this month as you are feeling spontaneous and up for fun and laughter – you will do your best to spark your partner into a similar frame of mind. You are motivated to socialize, and this can mean fun time for you and your partner as long as you don't flirt too much, OK!

CAREER

It is not with much enthusiasm that you are dealing with routine work commitments this month: if you work in admin, technology, medicine or IT you may feel less inspired. This is, however, a very good month to make a good impression on clients/customers or on your boss, and so even if the work is rather dull, you should use your personal magnetism and charm to influence those you work with in a positive way: win more clients and deal more effectively with colleagues and superiors. You have so much to give this month in terms of a positive and helpful attitude that no matter what line of work you are in, you can help make the day go quicker and things run more smoothly within teams.

In any business, look to cement good relationships with suppliers and others in your network – expand your list of contacts and use the drive you have right now to start new business relationships in your supply chain or distribution network. This is also a very good time to manage your image and that of your business – may you need a new logo or slogan. Get in touch with local business networkers who meet up or with your local chamber of commerce. Connecting via the internet is great, but in January you can gain an added advantage by networking the old way IN PERSON at events or business get-togethers. Do not be afraid of cold calling – pick up the phone and introduce yourself to prospective clients. Get new business cards printed and give them out at social and business gatherings – you can create magic by using your charisma this year, so start as you mean to go on.

Models, actors, presenters and those who use their image or persona to generate income can do exceedingly well this month – your business will grow, and there can be many lucrative new contracts.

Romance at the office is possible – but it may not go anywhere.

LIFE

It's a tale of the seven deadly sins this month, or at least six of them: greed, envy, pride, gluttony, sloth and lust. Depending on your point of view, this may sound like heaven, or indeed, hell. In many ways, your reactions to this month are a reflection of your psychological health and well-being. If you are in a position where you have good self-esteem and are feeling happy and contented, you will be generous, happy-go-lucky and ready to embrace life and others wholeheartedly; you will be magnanimous in victory and eager to share your spoils and share in the success of others, as well. If you are feeling insecure about yourself, you will experience envy and will be more inclined to spend conspicuously and seek attention in negative ways. You may spend excessively or eat and drink to excess to fulfil an inner emptiness. Perhaps you will come across as boastful or proud to deflect attention from the fact that you lack confidence. This month, you are putting up a front and perhaps going overboard to prove a point to others, when in reality, you are fooling no one but yourself.

If you can recognize why you are over compensating, you are well on the way to understanding. You must learn to love yourself and live for yourself according to your own unique values and destiny. Shun comparisons to others and revel in being your own special person with your own divine path in life. Fulfillment comes from within and not from material things or even from being loved. So don't resort to the deadly sins, you don't have to – be you and be proud of being you. Be the hero in your own movie not the bit part extra in someone else's.

LOVE

This is a very interesting month for love, romance and sex – you can certainly have a large helping of all three or perhaps a double of sex without the other two. Again, like the last paragraph it depends on how you feel about yourself, and if you want to let yourself go or whether you want to separate your body from your feelings for the sake of sex.

This can be a good month to let go and relax by enjoying sex for the physical sake of it – you may be seeking that moment of release rather than the emotional side that goes with it. However, if you are in a place where you feel emotionally ready for more, this is a time when sex can be the gateway to a whole new dimension in any relationship. Scorpios, either married or in long-term partnerships, have the opportunity to reach a new level of intimacy, both physical and spiritual in their relationships – there may be a deeper understanding or meaning that you are suddenly able to experience. Scorpios love to go deeper; they never skate on the surface, they always want more from any situation, and that includes people, lovers and relationships – so if you are with a Scorpio, this can be an exciting and surprising month.

For single Scorpios, some confusion may surround your love life – perhaps you get a Valentine card from someone and assume it is from someone else. You may get flowers from a mystery admirer, who is hoping you will guess who he/she is. It may be that the one you fancy is not quite what he seems, and you suddenly fall for someone completely different. Love is in the air but expect the unexpected.

CAREER

Musical and artistic ability are excellent and inspired this month – the muse is with you. Actors will have an enhanced ability to play a role and exude the emotion required. We are, however, all actors in this big production called life, and if you can act or use your acting skills in business, then that too is an advantage. You may just have an opportunity this month to gain a competitive edge or gain an advantage over colleagues by putting on a front or disguising expertly your real motivations like a poker player.

Investment in stocks, shares, art and precious metals/gemstones can be a wise move this month. Investments are intuitively led, and as long as you use caution alongside your gut feel, you can make a good decision.

This is a very good month for teachers and coaches, especially if you need to inspire your pupils or spot talent. As a teacher, you have a unique opportunity to identify talent in someone, and thereby change their life course for the better. Social workers can also be very effective this month, especially when guided by intuition, again you have a chance to make a difference.

If you are a working mom or dad, you may have to take time off work to deal with issues to do with your children.

This month is excellent for Scorpios who work in fields where intuition, compassion and instinct inform your decisions and guide you. In business, you may suss out an opportunity everyone else has missed. In every walk of life, it's about seeing what no one else sees and acting on that. It may also be believing in something that nothing objective can prove has worth, but which you instinctively feel is gold.

LIFE

I have been writing my series Horoscope 2015, and I cannot count how many times I have talked about ambitions, achievement, striving, hard work, reward, etc., etc. and I suddenly realized how little I have talked about fun. I think in the rat race we live in, we work hard and often play hard, but do we have fun? This March, Scorpios are rediscovering what fun means and how much fun contributes to well-being and also to spiritual understanding and evolvement.

While it's true that our work or career does not always fulfil us, it is often via hobbies and pastimes that we can connect with our true purpose or calling and feel a sense of meaning. This month is an ideal time to make time in your life to do the things that create meaning and allow you freedom to express yourself.

The solar eclipse in your fifth house gives an opportunity for the renewal of the life essence and enjoyment that replenishes the soul and gives meaning to your life. The emphasis this month will be on activities and spending your time in a way which is fun, and which nourishes you and renews your zest for life. Shake up the routine, break the mold and use this month to begin to live again.

Bonding with your children and finding fulfilment from your relationship with them is a feature of this month. If you do not have children, you may begin to long for a family and may make plans to start one. You could rediscover your youthfulness or sense of fun via children: your own or those you work with. Interaction with children could help you to rediscover a talent or ability.

LOVE

Look out single Scorpio as March is a time when a promising new romance can begin quite unexpectedly and take your world by storm.

Scorpios are feeling adventurous this month, and you guys are ready to embrace new relationships in a more gung ho fashion than usual. You may fall for someone who offers you something new – i.e. his interests or knowledge or where he comes from culturally intrigues and excites you. Relationships are the area where you want to expand, and so it makes sense that you will be attracted to lovers who can open doors for you in an intellectual and physical sense. This may well be a long distance relationship or one where you travel frequently together.

In ongoing relationships, you will be the one to initiate changes that can enhance your love life and also help you both to overcome difficulties in the relationship. This is an ideal time where your own positivity can change the course of the marriage/partnership and get it back on track to a happier and more fulfilling place for you both.

Looking at shared goals and making future plans which you will both work towards is key this month – you and your partner need to talk about your future together, your aims, dreams, ambitions, and then you need to talk about how to work towards those. Do not drift along, bogged down in routine and drudgery – think big, think about where you both want to be as a couple in the future. Create joint goals that can re-inspire the way you work together.

CAREER

Changes happening in your workplace may open doors for you career-wise. Things are very dynamic in your workplace or industry this year, nothing can be taken for granted; however, if you are alert, these changes could lead to new opportunities for you to change job or advance your career. Look to take on different responsibilities at work; if you are asked to do a slightly different role, grab that chance and show how well you can do at it. You are ready for more leadership and more responsibility now, take every chance you have to learn new skills, especially technical and scientific ones.

This is a very good month for Scorpios who work with technology or in enterprise development. March is an excellent time for Scorpios who work in alternate health and medicine fields to promote their business and educate the public more about your field of expertise – hold free workshops and seminars to create awareness and stimulate business.

Scorpios involved in sports or art forms that are physical i.e. dance, drama, ballet, gymnastics, etc. must pay more attention to diet – it is not about putting on weight, but finding a diet that suits you and helps you get more energy, more endurance and better recovery after events, i.e. Paleo Diet or Alkaline Diet.

LIFE

This can be a great month, where a burst of optimism and confidence can help get you over a hurdle, or it can also be a time when you throw caution to the wind and act unadvisedly, confident that you can get away with it – do not fall into the latter category. Temper some of your optimism with caution and do not make hasty decisions. You are impatient and prone to act rashly on the spur of the moment, take a step back and a deep breath – do not assume arrogantly that you have the answers. You can do yourself more harm than good by rushing into things. This is a good month to tackle issues head on, but not without thought and timing.

Impatience is a big problem this month as is frustration and boredom; you must find constructive and positive ways to burn up all your energy. Again, this is a good month to try new things, especially physical exercise and sports, as long as you heed the general advice of the month not to overdo it.

Try not to exaggerate anything, and do not promise more than you can deliver; you have big plans and the benefit of foresight right now, but you are not very good with details and are prone to overlook anything which does not fit into your vision. Don't shun advice from others and try and take the ideas of others on board as they may have more value than you think.

You are keen to be seen as someone with influence and to be respected in your field/community; you can indeed win that respect as long as you are not too keen or over eager. In trying to stand out from others, you may alienate those you seek to gain respect and cooperation from – cooperate with and respect others, and you can achieve far more.

LOVE

Passionate and energetic, you are amorous and sexual this month. There may also be battles of wills with your partner, and you will fight your corner hard; you are feisty and not willing to back down. Your red-blooded attitude is great for your sex life but may not bode well for general household harmony with arguments breaking out.

You need your freedom this month; you may grab the keys and storm off enigmatically after an argument to clear your head. Things are not that serious, you really just need to let off steam and clear the air – partners of Scorpio are best advised to let you go and cool off and not try and reason too hard with you. Scorpios often like to have their say and then slam the door and simmer down for a few hours. Scorpios don't always want to hear the other side until later when they have calmed down.

Lovemaking and calm should resume quite quickly after an outburst.

Single Scorpio want to be challenged this month – Scorpios love partners who push their buttons and test them, Passionate arguments may be a sign the new relationship is actually going well.

CAREER

Again, caution is the keyword – over-optimism may lead you to take a risk or make an unwise choice this month, especially financially.

This is a very good month for forward planning where your vision, ideas and leadership are key. However, you need to work better with others who can help flush out the details of the plans and see things that you have overlooked.

This is a month where you care deeply about what you do, and you have the power to inspire your colleagues and get them more involved and committed. You may quickly lose patience with workmates or clients who are lackluster and unresponsive, and you need to withdraw from these people or try and ignore them as they can get you very wound up.

You may be the driving force behind recruiting new staff or tendering for new services. Things at work may be quite cutthroat with some hard decisions having to be made – you can make these decisions, and you can also help with the adjustments.

Changes in your field or within your firm are good for you right now, and these changes are actually what you need to help you progress and find more fulfilment at work.

LIFE

You are in a creative and innovative mood – you welcome new ideas and can be quick to change your mind about things as new information comes to light. This is not the time to be stuck in your ways as events will challenge you to defend your views and move with the times. Some may find you erratic as you may appear to be chopping and changing between this thing, and that. It is certainly a month of fast-paced activity, and you will not have much time to relax.

Scorpios love to broach taboo subjects, and you may use this month to bring up some truths that everyone else is steering clear of – you may stir up controversy by saying what others are thinking. My advice is to think about whether you can handle the heat before you turn it up – it may be worth it in the long run, but do make a calculated choice before wading in on any controversial topic.

This can be an irritating month when people seem to get in your way for no good reason, creating what you see as unnecessary problems. It will mainly be people in bureaucratic positions or in the civil service who cause you trouble – try and be diplomatic, but keep the pressure on.

This is not a month for self-discipline, and so if you are on a diet or training for something, make allowances and cut back in April, so you don't feel too bad. Do not leave yourself with too many deadlines for May as it will be hard to muster up the determination and concentration levels to achieve what you need to do. This is a great month for errands, communicating, learning new things and local travel.

There will be many social engagements, i.e. parties and other celebrations, and this will put you into a fun-loving, carefree frame of mind.

LOVE

Your needs in your relationship are changing, but is your partner keeping up? You and your loved one's needs may be at odds this month, and it can be hard to strike a balancing act.

Emotions can run high this month, and it may not be easy for you to see his/her point of view – you may be accused of not being sensitive enough. It is likely that you will say something that seems obvious to you, but is perceived as being very hurtful to the other person. This can be the problem: what you see as hurtful is not what your partner sees as hurtful/insulting and vice versa. This can mean that passions become inflamed over things that you each say without meaning to be taken as badly as they are. Respect runs both ways: you demand it, and you must give it. However, it is not that simple as your definitions of respect are very different – this is where you need to listen more and make an effort to understand what hurt your loved one and how they interpret respect.

Do not go overboard giving your partner what they do not want – sometimes what you enjoy giving is not what your partner enjoys receiving. It boils down to understanding each other's needs better and being willing to accommodate them. You are highly aware of psychic undercurrents in the relationship right now, and that can make you suspicious; please keep things in proportion.

Single Scorpio are very idealistic in love and may be prepared to make sacrifices for a partner whom they have only known a short time – do not let your heart run away totally unrestrained, allow your head a say.

All relationships can be rather extreme right now – swinging from love to hate and back again, but there certainly is passion and fire.

CAREER

Scorpios work best where they are emotionally involved in the job. In jobs where this is the case, you can work tirelessly and almost obsessively to achieve results this month. Your work is also very personal to you, and you will defend your ideas and your projects pugnaciously.

Artistically, Scorpios can produce work of great drama and flair this May. Those who write books, articles, columns, etc. may aim to be shocking and provocative in what they say to get people talking. An excellent month for movie makers, playwrights and writers of fiction.

It is a very effective month for those in politics or speech writing where mass communication of ideas and the ability to rouse an audience is important – you have the power to use words to manipulate and engender a response. Scorpio bankers, stockbrokers, investors and those who handle others' money must be very cautious this month – do not take risks.

A lack of objectivity and a tendency to be emotionally involved to too great a degree can impair your judgment, and you must try and be more detached and listen to advice this month.

Both women and men can use sexual tactics to gain an advantage or make an impression at work – use this by all means, but do keep control as it can be a tactic with a downside.

LIFE

Pay close attention to your dreams this month as they may hold clues about your future, your subconscious or what you should be paying attention to in your life. Sometimes, dreams are just a product of indigestion and are pure nonsense, but often they hold meaning, especially if they reoccur, and they are worth investigating. There may also be coincidences or feelings of déjà vu – it is a very psychic month when you are drawn to interpret the unseen and the hidden meanings in things. You have a keen imagination this month and can apply this to all your artistic pursuits.

In any walk of life, your power to think beyond the obvious and the practical can be very helpful.

Your appreciation of poetry, music and the esoteric is enhanced right now and visits to theatre, concerts and art galleries can be more informative and even spiritually awakening. Scorpios are usually deeply spiritual, and they seek meaning through often extreme circumstances in life; even when they claim to be atheists, they are just as in need of explanations, be it scientific or otherwise – this month that need to find a meaning or an interpretation for your life can lead you to churches, mosques, libraries, ancient ruins or séances.

You are highly intuitive right now and ideally placed to give advice to people, especially young and vulnerable people. You can pick up on subtle hints and signs which can enable you a unique insight into others' problems.

LOVE

A very romantic time when you can get close to your partner with little notes, surprise presents, flowers, candlelit dinners, musical gifts etc. – you are very thoughtful right now and can really enhance your love life with meaningful gestures and kind words.

Kindness is actually a keyword in love – a little understanding goes a very long way. What your loved one needs now is a hug, a reassuring smile and a supportive hand on the arm; what she/he does not need is criticism and detailed advice. Sometimes too much advice is a bad thing, often all someone wants is to feel understood and not judged, and that is where Scorpio can excel this month – you are able to say the right thing at the right time to make your partner feel better and more confident and optimistic.

This is a very good month for all love relationships as you are so intuitive and understanding; you are also able to emit a calming and relaxing influence, which bodes well for romantic and meaningful sex. Sex this month is about a spiritual connection and experiencing true feeling, it is far more than lust and physical satisfaction.

CAREER

This is an ideal month to get loans or negotiate loan agreements – you are well placed to make a good impression, and you are able to get through the process no matter how complicated as you have energy and determination,

In general, this is a good time to tackle your taxes (business or personal), deal with creditors, barter for better deals on overdrafts or repayments or rearrange your investments – you have the energy to deal with these financial issues right now, and so you should seize the opportunity and see what savings could be made. It is not a good time to borrow from friends or where there is no formal agreement – don't do anything on a handshake, no matter what terms you and the other party are on personally, get it all tied up legally.

June is the time to make a good impression: make sure you promote your business and your products this month, be bold and be visible, and do not hold back on boasting about your achievements. This is a very good time to look for a job if you are unemployed as you can create a favorable impact on an employer. Be creative about how you apply for jobs, do not rely on websites and recruitment services

– go in person and introduce yourself to a prospective employer and hand over your CV. Make telephone calls to firms/companies who employ people with your skills and ask about opportunities, even offer to work for free for a few days a week or to temp. Think about how to make yourself visible to employers and how you can stand out from the rest.

LIFE

Friendships are important to you and yet keeping the peace among your friends can be hard. You may have to play go-between, and even this role could be complicated due to misunderstandings – encourage direct communication and try not to be the messenger or you will get caught in crossfire.

This month you have courage, decisiveness and willpower – you can make very good decisions as you can see all sides and can weigh options with clear judgment. You can get a lot done as you have mental energy and stamina. However, perhaps it is the effect of the summer holidays (if you are in the Northern Hemisphere) approaching, making you feel rather laid back and not very motivated, which will cause you not to make as much of this time as you could. It may work the opposite way in that the thought of your holiday or time off approaching gives you a surge of energy that allows you to achieve a massive amount in quick time. Don't waste the energy you have this month – get outside, get active, get the endorphins going and use this time to tackle new projects.

There is a strong sense of honor and integrity, and nothing is too much trouble for you when it comes to lending a hand and helping someone out, or standing up for someone.

LOVE

Friendships can often turn into love this month and so be on the lookout for those in your friendship circle who may also be ready for a budding romance. You may be introduced to someone new via a friend; blind dates are also possible.

On the flipside, do be careful that a close friend does not get the wrong idea and think that you want more; it can be hard to resume the friendship once a certain line has been crossed.

Taking yourself too seriously can hamper relations with your partner – you are torn between the need to have fun and move on, and yet nagging doubts, fears and resentments keep surfacing and you cannot shake them off. Deeper issues in the relationship are troubling you even though on the surface everything is rolling along nicely; this can translate as an unwillingness to experience intimacy and a certain coolness and detachment when you are alone with your partner. Things go really well when you are with friends and family, but when alone as a couple, conversation is forced – it's maybe you who just has to get over yourself and release these doubts. Nothing can be perfect, but while you cling to issues, no future without those issues is possible. Everyone else has moved on and so must you – life has no reverse on forward.

CAREER

This is a month when experience counts – projects and knowledge gained from past jobs can be crucial in unpicking and working out how to handle difficult problems and complex tasks.

This is a very good month for Scorpio in politics who wish to reform and even revolutionize – if you are on the cutting edge of liberalism or human rights, you can create awareness and this can be very successful for campaigning and changing minds.

Technological advancement is key this month, and even if you are not a technically minded person you should try and incorporate as many new IT solutions as you can to streamline your work and keep up with the competition.

For Scorpios, who work in science and technology, this is a month when you can make excellent progress and gain recognition from your peers. The hardest thing this month is gaining acceptance for your ideas – you will have to work hard to convince others to see your plans are workable and that their time has come.

They say there is nothing more powerful than an idea whose time has come, and this month Scorpio are at the forefront of those ideas.

This month you may decide to put in for a transfer or find an opportunity to move between departments – there are opportunities to gain more responsibility and move up in order to earn more money within your current career. When the time comes, do not turn it down – you have the ability and can cope easily with the step up.

LIFE

Resourceful and full of determination, you can change yourself and the world around you – it is not a month of accepting things or leaving your life in fate's hands. You know that no one can help you get where you want to be, but you, and all it takes is the first step. There is a steel resolve and also an excitement within you – you want to move into a new phase of life and can see the opportunity now arising. Sometimes it feels as if all doors are closed and we are in one huge cul-de-sac, but this month you can see that doors are opening and your own mindset is also changing and allowing you to accept changes that you may have shied away from before.

It is a very good time to reflect on significant aspects of your past and to see them now in a new light – what can you learn from them? Learn the lesson and let those experiences go. This is an important part of your year of transformation, where you can live with more freedom by letting go of past events that have affected your psychology and your behavior in the present. This is not a month of severe breaks with the past; more of a happy waving goodbye as the past drifts off like a boat into the ocean of oblivion.

You will be drawn to activities both in work and within hobbies and recreation, which test you mentally and physically – you will seek to prove to yourself how much you can achieve and how far you can go. It is a month of personal goal setting and goal achievement. Some of these goals may be so personal that no one even knows about them; others may be more public, but no one will know the relevance to you personally.

LOVE

Attitudes in sex and love are inextricably linked to your experience with your mother this month. If your mother was loving and supportive, you will have a smooth and positive month within communications and sexual matters in your love life. You will find it easy to give, share and let go emotionally both in new and older relationships.

However, if you had a mother who was critical, unloving or vague, then you may well have internalized messages about yourself which are negative and which can impact your current relationship or even long-term relationship formation. Scorpio children must have strong emotional attachment figures whom they trust and who give them love, boundaries and emotional support. When this does not happen, Scorpios can have problems later on with intimacy and with allowing themselves to let go and trust.

This month Scorpios should look to their relationship with Mom, to see how this is impacting on their self-esteem and their current relationships.

CAREER

You are very impressive in the way you handle authority this month – having authority can be somewhat of a poison chalice as people tend to resent those with power; however, you are able to use the power you have in a very positive and inclusive way, which will earn you respect.

You can be very persuasive as your strong inner convictions shine through – people are far more likely to buy into what you are saying or selling if you are a walking advert for it and are putting your money where your mouth is, so to speak. Whatever you teach about or preach about, you will find an audience who are receptive as your charisma and obvious enthusiasm for what you are saying is clear.

This is a month of concrete action and results – you will strive towards achieving quantifiable results, and you will be successful. It is a good month to work on aspects of your business that are easy to compare and contrast, i.e. sales, profit, new clients, cost reduction, higher royalties, better feedback etc., rather than areas like employee relations, advertising results, creativity which are impossible to either quantify or compare. Put your effort into the nuts and bolts of the business. In a job, work on results your boss can actually see, do not waste time on things he/she won't realize you have done.

A very good month for Scorpios who work in research or investigation, i.e. police work, forensics, investigative journalism, geology, audit and law. An incisive mind allows you to detect what is important in a mass of red herrings.

LIFE

Be prepared for some disruption to your life that is beyond your control. Scorpios like to be in control; you do not like surprises and this month you are going to have to roll with it. Some of the surprising events this month can be seen as the universe trying to draw your attention to something that you have either pushed to the recesses of your mind or ignored totally. Problems you have avoided can often crop up now in unexpected ways and demand to be dealt with.

It may be the case that you suddenly, without warning, reach the end of your tether on a matter, and in effect throw the baby out with the bathwater in an attempt to free yourself of the problem. You will be inclined to speak and act rashly, and thus things can come to a head quite quickly. It is not a month of holding back.

You know how sometimes you feel something brewing, or you have this feeling of tension as if the storm is about to break – this month it is Scorpio who may act to precipitate or bring on what is on the verge of happening, almost as if you have to act out what others are holding back on.

You have strong opinions and are not in a compromising mood. It is quite possible that you will have some secret or damaging information that you have to decide how to handle. The way you communicate and what you choose to reveal and when, can have long-lasting and perhaps even serious consequences.

Delay travel and in routine travel be very cautious as accidents are a possibility this month.

LOVE

Single Scorpio may well attract a love interest who has similar interests and ideas to you and who can both encourage and improve on your ideas and plans. The more you can bounce ideas off each other, the better the relationship.

Over-eagerness and expectations which are unrealistic can be a problem in all relationships both new and old. There is a mismatch of desire this month with you wanting one thing and your partner being in a totally different mindset will be wanting another. It can be hard to coordinate yourselves to experience romance and to click physically.

You may feel that you are doing all the loving and giving, and your partner may feel that he/she is giving in a slightly different way. It can be hard for you both to appreciate or place value on what the other is doing, even if you are both doing most things right.

Clashes about how to bring up the kids, how to spend household income, where and if to go on holiday and also arguments to do with each other's sets of friends can be an issue, these issues will not result in a major argument, but an atmosphere can develop.

CAREER

This is a very good month for Scorpio in building, civil engineering, business management, accounting and property law. However, for any Scorpio it is a very good time of year for pursuing career landmarks and ambitions – you may want to study for another qualification to enhance your prospects or reputation, or you may ask for a transfer to a different position to gain more experience.

Changes in career right now can have an impact on your life, i.e. moving home, travelling to work in a different way, new wardrobe, you may need to get more fit to pass the medical, etc. There are some personal changes you will have to make right now to aid you in your new work role or career.

You are very well organized and methodical right now, which will help you to cope with a large volume of work systematically. You are well equipped right now to manage money, and you should be lucky with money – in your business you will cover costs and turn a profit, and in your personal life you will be able to cover expenses and even set money aside.

An important month to manage your pension or even get some professional advice on your pension savings and how to get more out of savings. If you have not started a pension, think about it now.

You have a high degree of self-discipline, which can aid you immensely in all physical and sporting endeavors – you can push through the pain and tiredness with focus and determination.

Despite your strong individual opinions, you can take orders from superiors and carry them out to the letter, which will earn you credit.

LIFE

Your thinking is strongly influenced by habits and impulsive reactions fueled by the subconscious. If you always eat when you are lonely or go shopping when you are blue then this month it will be harder to curb those habits; likewise, if you have given up smoking you may find it harder to resist the temptation of a ciggie this month. Much of the way you react to situations is compulsive and may not be logical, and your decision-making is also highly subjective and even biased, so it is not the best time to make critical choices.

You can be rather coy and secretive – you are a dark horse and may keep your true feelings secret, which can be a very helpful thing.

This month you will seek refuge from the madding crowd – Scorpio is a sign who values seclusion and privacy, even if you have strong influences from signs like Gemini and Leo you will still need periods of quiet where you keep you own council and enjoy your own company. Rest and quiet contemplation are vital for your mental health this month; it is almost as if you have to recharge your batteries by just cutting yourself off from the rat race. You may book a weekend away to somewhere quiet by a lake or in the mountains, or perhaps you will curl up with a book and lock the door. It is a time you need to escape with your imagination into another world.

In all health related issues, REST is the key. If you do get the flu or have another kind of health problem right now, it is a message to you to slow down and get much-needed rest. A bout of flu may be just what you need to give yourself an excuse to have that much-needed break.

LOVE

If you and your partner are very close, you can use this month to escape together on a romantic break away from the kids, your friends and your family. If you have felt as if your partner has been invading your space, this may be the ideal time to spend a little quality time apart – absence makes the heart grow fonder.

Escapism and fantasy are very important for your sex life this month – you must break the routine and recapture the romance with music, movies and even love letters to each other. Do not overanalyze yourself or your partner, the best thing this month is to let go of everything – fears, worries, anxieties and guilt – allow yourself freedom to enjoy yourself and be carefree. Leave your problems outside of the bedroom door and make sure your love life is an impenetrable bubble of love and bliss, one part of your life free of hassle and worry.

Also, let go of an obsession with details and being perfect in every way – nothing is perfect, and imperfections are actually quite intriguing and sexy. Embrace who you are and accept yourself in every way, this will aid all your love relationships new and old, and intimacy can reach a new level.

CAREER

Scorpios form strong bonds and lasting friendships with work colleagues, and this month those friendships are especially rewarding and fun. You may make new friends at work, and the camaraderie and shared experience of working towards goals with others make work a pleasure.

This is a very good month for Scorpios who work in careers where your achievements affect wider society and your community: this may be political activism, social work, humanitarian work, nursing, animal welfare or green campaigns. You can communicate effectively and get more exposure for your work, which can help bring in funds and further your aims.

It is important for those who run businesses to be mindful of issues like the environment, employment law and fairness and equality in the workplace. If you are an employee, you may be instrumental in helping or encouraging those you work with to be greener, open-minded and more socially aware and active.

In October, you can steal a march on your competitors (in business or within your firm) by being a little out there – do not be afraid to innovate and embrace the wild and wacky.

LIFE

Excellent timing in both business and romantic relationships is yours. You are in the right place at the right time to make contacts and meet people who can be fortuitous for you both financially and socially.

Good karma these next few months is a result of past friendship and generosity of spirit.

There is a feel good factor this month; however, you should not let this feeling that all is well lead you to be frivolous and squander money unnecessarily.

Freedom is important to you, and you will be abrupt with those who seek to waste your time and curtail your freedom of thought and movement. Honesty and being who you are and saying what you mean really matters to you – falseness and empty smiles will have no sway with you, you want to cut straight to the heart of the matter with no insincere niceties. Scorpios are not beating about the bush; you are getting things done and letting nothing get in your way.

LOVE

You are selfless and devoted this month, and your relationships will fare very well as you are putting a lot of work and effort in communication and into the day-to-day matters where you share responsibility. You can also help your partner in a practical way, i.e. with their workload, with their accounts, with their diet or in meeting deadlines. It's a month of putting your money where your mouth is when it comes to expressing care and concern: it isn't just about saying you care, it's about jumping in with some concrete assistance, and this will go a long way to making your loved one feel secure and loved. This all bodes well for the relationship. Saying you care is one thing – showing it takes it to a whole new dimension.

Scorpio are very sincere in love and relationships and will not say what they do not feel – if they say "I love you" right now, they mean it as they will not go along with anything their heart is not in.

Scorpios in new relationships or who are dating will want clarity, any evasiveness or game playing will turn them off instantly. They will say what they mean, and they expect the same back – no slushy insincere romantic talk will woo a Scorpio in November.

CAREER

Deals struck now can pay dividends for some time to come. This is a very good time to strike agreements and to make breakthroughs in negotiations. A great month to find new clients and develop new working relationships in your business.

Transport and delivery problems can cause havoc this month, and so do track important parcels, and if transport is a vital part of your business, get deliveries out ahead of schedule. If you drive for a living take extra care and ensure your car is equipped for extreme weather.

The next few months will be very inspirational for those of you who work in fields where inspiration and feel have much to do with your work: this can be art, sports and even gambling (regular gamblers who gamble anyway will have good luck, I am not recommending taking up gambling).

This is a wonderful and productive time for Scorpios in the healing professions or who undertake charity work – you will gain a real sense of achievement and fulfilment from your work.

LIFE

Highly idealistic, you are driven to set yourself goals for the New Year which reflect the very best of who you are and what you can be. Doing things for others and making this Holiday Season special is important to you, you may even volunteer somewhere to help people who are ill, homeless or destitute this Christmas to have a better time and even a better start to next year. For you, this Christmas is not all about you and being materialistic, it is far more about company, nostalgia, sharing, caring and the joy of giving. Your desire to help others and to be part of something worthwhile is a driver in many of the things you do this month.

You may be drawn to water this month – the seaside, a log cabin by the lake, walks by the river. Water sports, sailing or simply reading a book on the beach is an ideal way to relax and get in touch with your inner emotions. You can make very good decisions when you are near or on the water. You may well start a new hobby involving water.

Once again, having fun and enjoying whatever you do is central – if you are not enjoying something, you won't stick it out. The more you enjoy yourself, the more of yourself you can give.

LOVE

Single Scorpios are far more interested in platonic relationships this month – if you have recently started a new love affair, you may cool it off and try to develop the friendship side first. It is very important for you to have a connection with the person you are dating, and that means feeling you can be honest and share with them as a friend – if you feel that the friendship element is not there, you may cool things off.

This is a very good month for marriages and partnerships as long as you do not feel controlled or inhibited – this is a time when you are free to give love and support generously. However, as soon as you feel curtailed or bossed around in any way, you will get your back up and could react quite dramatically.

Scorpios are not interested in routine and in living a boxed-in life right now: they want to be impulsive and follow whims and dreams, they want to be imaginative and spontaneous – a partner who goes with this will have a great time, but a stick-in-the-mud who does not want anything new will get left behind. Your Scorpio partner wants life to be full of life, and so you had better adapt or die as they say.

CAREER

Very careful and systematic, you are methodical and precise and can handle a vast volume of work. A very good month for Scorpio for whom Christmas is a very important and busy time of year i.e. in retail, hospitality, entertainment and leisure.

Full of energy and enthusiasm, you can bring the year to a very successful conclusion workwise.

December is ideal for detail work, communications and productivity. If you make things, you can produce more products and more designs. You can coordinate activities, make lists and pay attention to vital details others have missed. Although much of your work will be behind the scenes, you are the vital team member who holds it together.

Scorpios organizing events or those who teach or coach sporting teams can be very successful. In fact, success is almost guaranteed in a venture this month.

Everyone can rely on you, and you relish this responsibility – you will take much pride from your performance in December, and it's thanks to you that things go as well as they do.

WELL DONE SCORPIO!

THANK YOU FOR PURCHASING THIS BOOK AND ALL THE VERY BEST FOR 2016!